THE
KING'S
WAY OF LIFE

Dedication

To my beautiful daughters: May you always hide wisdom in your heart so that you may know the right thing to do and become all you're destined to be. (Psalm 119:11) I love you so much.
—Brandon Walden

To our Dads
—Kevin & Kristen Howdeshell

This book belongs to:

DESTINY IMAGE® PUBLISHERS, INC.

P.O. Box 310, Shippensburg, PA 17257-0310

"Promoting Inspired Lives."

This book and all other Destiny Image and Destiny Image Fiction books are available at Christian bookstores and distributors worldwide.

For more information on foreign distributors, call 717-532-3040.

Or reach us on the Internet: www.destinyimage.com

ISBN 13 HC: 978-0-7684-5110-8
ISBN 13 EBook: 978-0-7684-5109-2
ISBN 13 TP: 978-0-7684-5264-8
For Worldwide Distribution, Printed in the U.S.A.

1 2 3 4 5 6 7 8 9 10 11 / 27 26 25 24 23 22 21 20

THE
KING'S
WAY OF LIFE

This is a tale of the king and his sons
in the kingdom their family was chosen to run.
The king was no more, and the people were sad.
Their father had died. The sons lost their dad.

Both sons had been given, their very first day,
a necklace and compass to show them the way.
The compass was placed on a chain near their heart.
It was worn in the light. It was worn in the dark.

Their father was kind, and he never caused strife.
He'd shown them that he knew the king's way of life.
The king's way of life was leading while serving,
being kind and generous to those undeserving.

"Rule like a servant and serve like a king.
Lifting up others is the best thing."

These were the words the king spoke every day,
his message, the motto, that he always would say.
They'd seen him show it, time and again.
"If you live like me," he said, "you'll always win."

The king had ruled with wisdom and grace,
wearing his compass through all of his days.
His compass had led him, his kingdom had grown.
But now his two boys were left on their own.

The king's elder son, whose first name was Thomas,
was prone to deceit and could not keep a promise.
But William, the younger, was more like his father.
The king's way of life was never a bother.

Now, Thomas, the elder, had chosen early on
to be selfish and stingy and to do things all wrong.
He loved all the wealth that came to a royal,
but unlike his brother, was mean and disloyal.

He traded his compass for diamonds and jewels.
He could not be trusted. He made his own rules.
The younger brother was more like the king.
Helping his people made his young heart sing.

William was humble and generous, too.
His compass had shown him all that he should do.
The compass had helped him with every decision.
He consulted it daily. He trusted its vision.

North told him "Yes,"

and South was a "No."

East meant "Go fast,"

and West said "Go Slow."

The compass had proven, time and again.
It was not only a compass, but also a friend.

Then came the day for a king to be crowned,
but Thomas, the elder, was not to be found.
He had left in a hurry during the dark night.
He had fully rejected the king's way of life.

The nobles said William was now to be king.
This was not something he had foreseen.
William lacked zeal. He had questions and doubted.
Inside his mind, his worries all shouted:

"Would I be enough?
And how would I lead?
Would I rule like my father?
And would I succeed?

"Would father have waited?
Would he have walked away,
and run from his destiny,
or chosen to stay?"

While nervously pacing, he dropped his device,
the compass that showed him the king's way of life.
Shattered and broken it lay on the floor.
The gift from his father now was no more.

He couldn't rule now, William was sure.
Not when the future was so insecure.
He gathered the kingdom and told them his rule
would not continue, he'd been a fool.

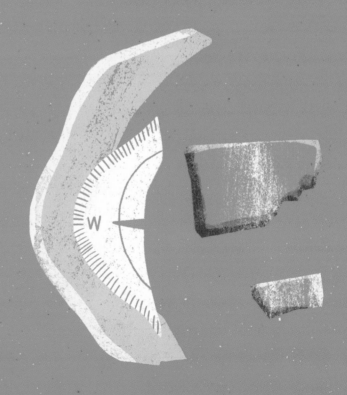

So, the town held a meeting. Three men did apply.
Men stepped up from the masses who weren't shy.
The first man to arrive had such strength in each arm,
but his power was just used to cause others harm.

The next to apply was quite rich and greedy.
And he did not share what he had with the needy.
The last who applied was loud and compelling,
but he spent all his campaigning time yelling.

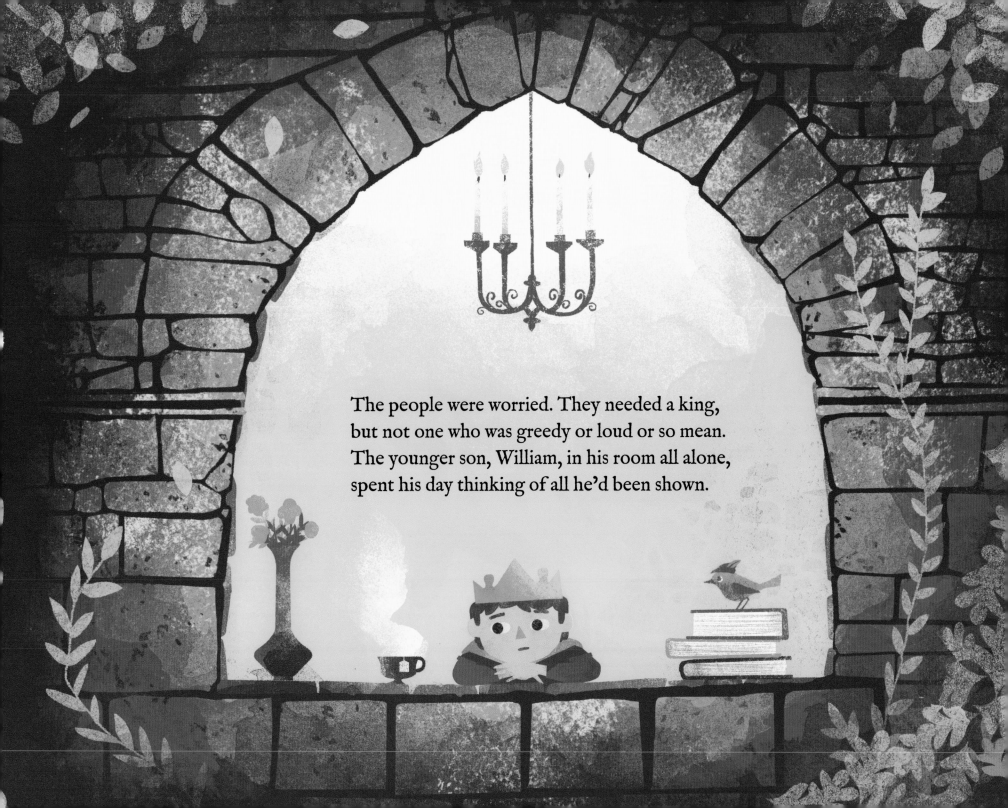

The people were worried. They needed a king,
but not one who was greedy or loud or so mean.
The younger son, William, in his room all alone,
spent his day thinking of all he'd been shown.

The guards then announced, "Now, the votes are all in."
But none who applied was the one to win.
William, the younger, had won the town's vote.
His name was the one that the people all wrote.

The people all trusted young William's decisions.
They knew the young king would now have a vision.
The kingdom rejoiced. They now had a king.
The music had started. The people would sing.

But the humble new king spent his first night concerned.
He tried to remember the motto he'd learned.
He woke in the morning, like each day before,
but was not prepared for what was in store.

His compass was gone. It was broken to pieces.
He thought to himself, "Now how can I lead us?"
William felt lost. "My compass is gone.
It always showed answers that I relied on."

He thought to himself, "Oh, what shall I do?
If only dear Father had left me a clue."
And just like that these words came to mind,
the same ones he'd heard hundreds of times.

"Rule like a servant and serve like a king.
Lifting up others is the best thing."

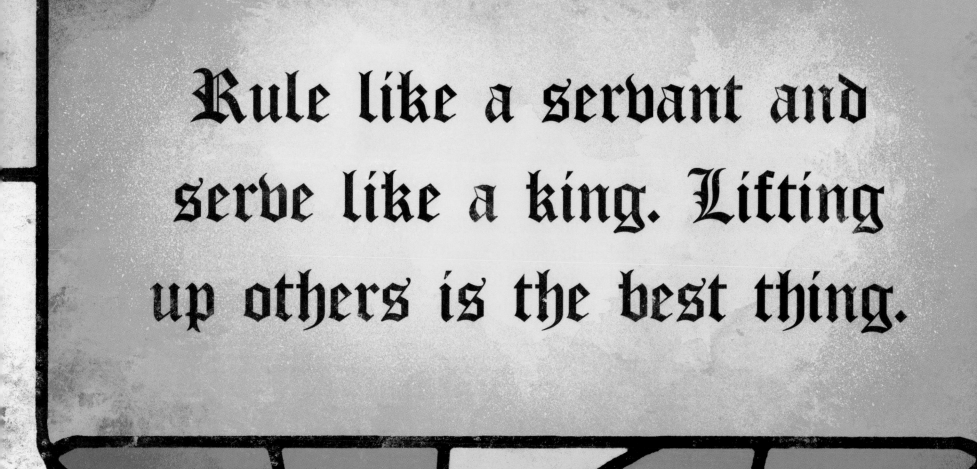

Rule like a servant and serve like a king. Lifting up others is the best thing.

The compass was in him. He'd kept wisdom close.
He'd lead like his father through highs and through lows.
But his people lacked wisdom, and he thought of their plight.
They depended on his words and the king's way of life.

William went away quietly, his hand near his heart,
where the necklace and compass were from the start.
As he held his hand there and he looked to the tower,
He thought of a way he could use his power.

So, he called the chief jeweler and spared no expense.
His people would each have a compass, a friend.

They'd each gain wisdom through their device.
They each could now choose the king's way of life.

Then came the day that Thomas returned.
He was bruised and battered from the lessons he'd learned.
William forgave him and did not cause strife.
He gave him a gift, the king's way of life.

So remember, whenever you've gone astray
or it feels as though you can't find your way,
the king's way of life will be your guide.
It's a motto, a compass, a friend on your side.

The End.

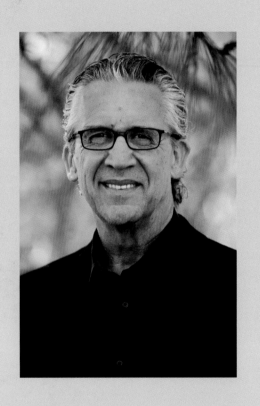

Bill Johnson is a fifth-generation pastor with a rich heritage in the Holy Spirit. Bill and his wife, Beni, are the senior leaders of Bethel Church in Redding, California, and serve a growing number of churches that cross denominational lines, demonstrate power, and partner for revival. Bill's vision is for all believers to experience God's presence and operate in the miraculous—as expressed in his bestselling books *When Heaven Invades Earth* and *Hosting the Presence*. The Johnsons have three children and ten grandchildren.

Brandon Walden is a husband, father, bestselling author of *Seeds and Trees*, and a public speaker. He lives with his wife, Stephanie, and his 5 beautiful daughters in Redding, California. The Walden Family has travelled the US extensively sharing songs and stories of faith and family with audiences coast to coast. The Walden Family creates content and resources for parents, families, teachers and therapists to impact children and children at heart. Find out more about Brandon at www.brandonwalden.com or follow him @brandonwalden on Instagram.

Kevin & Kristen Howdeshell are a

husband and wife team illustrating a variety of projects including bestselling children's books, food packaging, movie posters, music albums, and editorial spots. Their work is characterized with texture, a mid-century influence and a lean toward meaningful family time. They lead up The Brave Union Studio in Kansas City, Missouri where they raise their three young kids, and enjoy their Betta fish, their treehouse, and trampoline. In their non-art-hours, Kevin enjoys fly fishing, Kristen likes working in the yard while listening to a baseball game, and board games with the kids. Follow their work @TheBraveUnion on instagram.